# THE BEATLES

## SESSION PARTS

Transcribed by Kevin Johnson

ISBN 978-1-4803-5357-2

### HAL•LEONARD® CORPORATION

7777 W. BLUEMOUND RD. P.O. BOX 13819 MILWAUKEE, WI 53213

Visit Hal Leonard Online at
**www.halleonard.com**

# CONTENTS

# ALL YOU NEED IS LOVE

Words and Music by John Lennon
and Paul McCartney

All you need is love     All you need is love     love

24

FADE OUT

# BLUE JAY WAY

Words and Music by
George Harrison

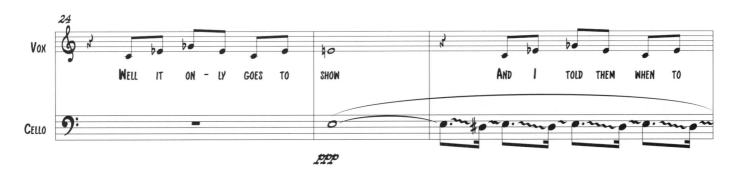

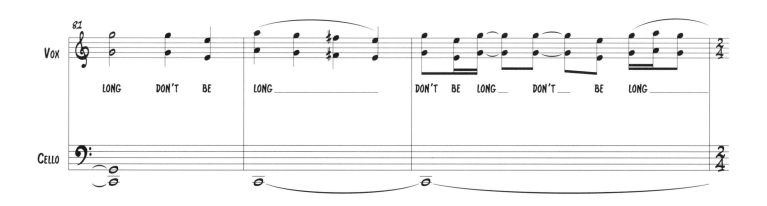

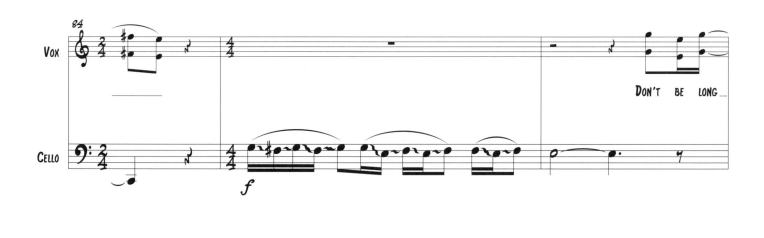

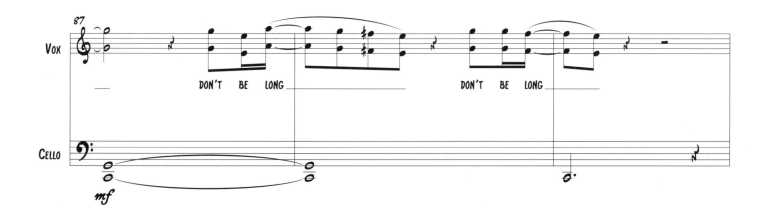

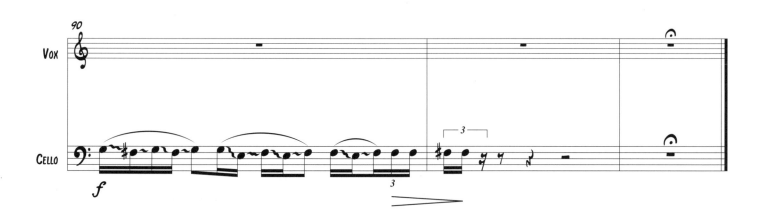

# ELEANOR RIGBY

Words and Music by John Lennon
and Paul McCartney

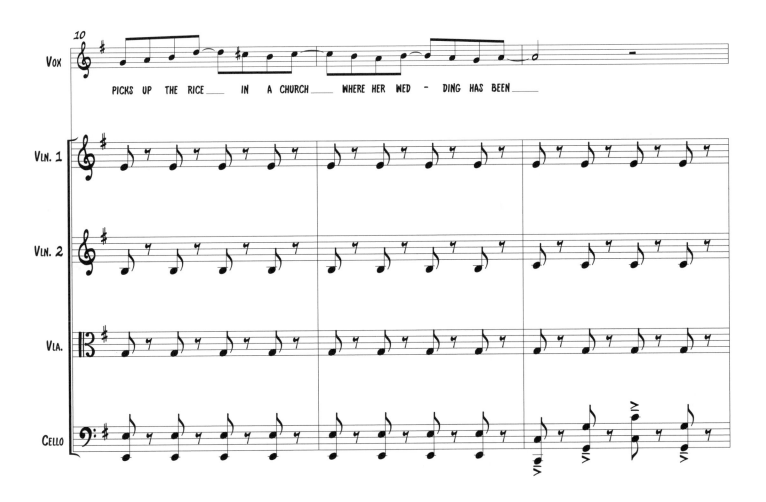

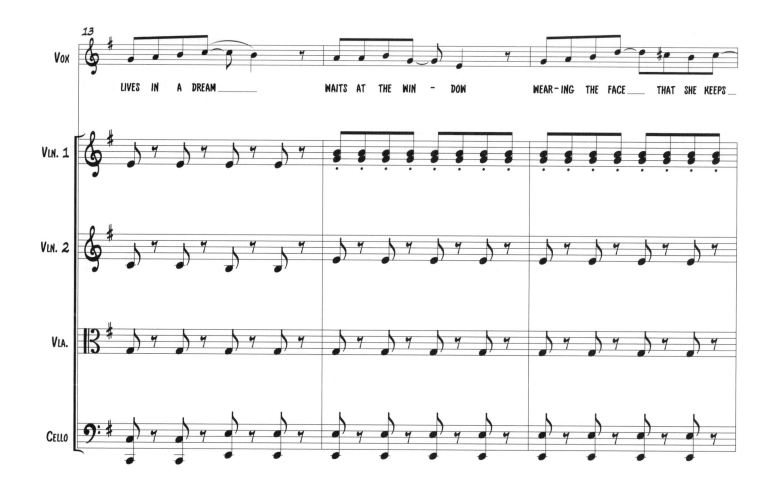

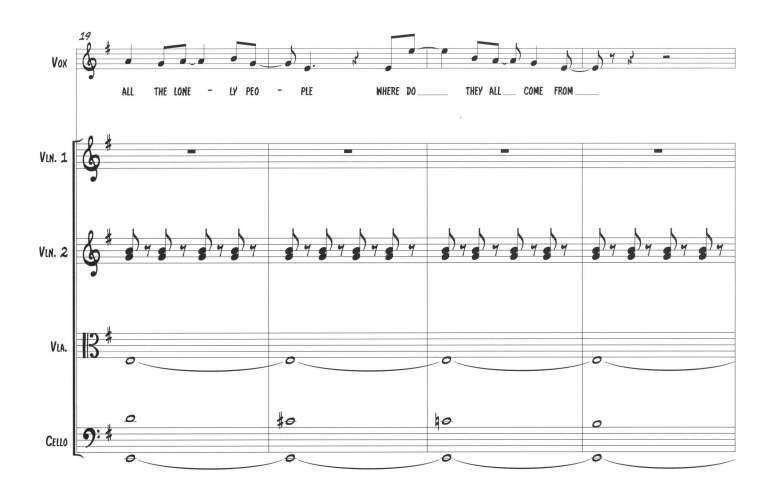

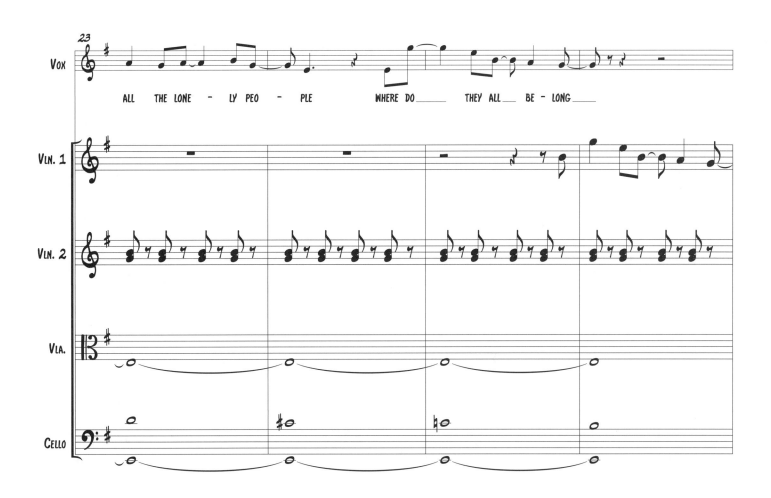

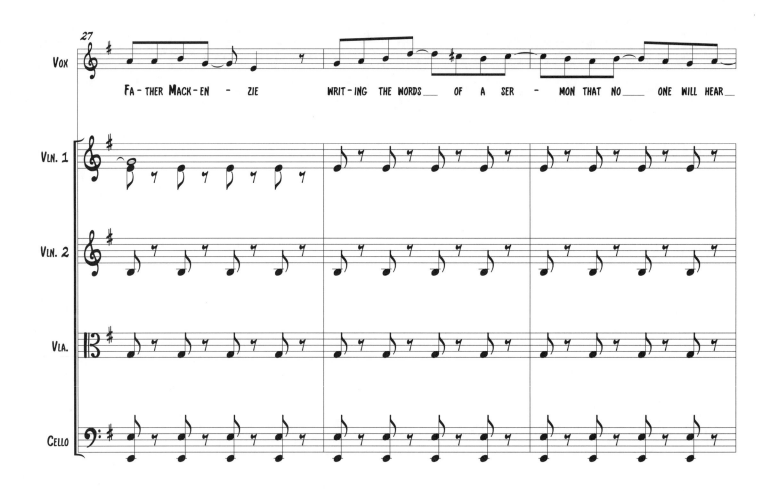

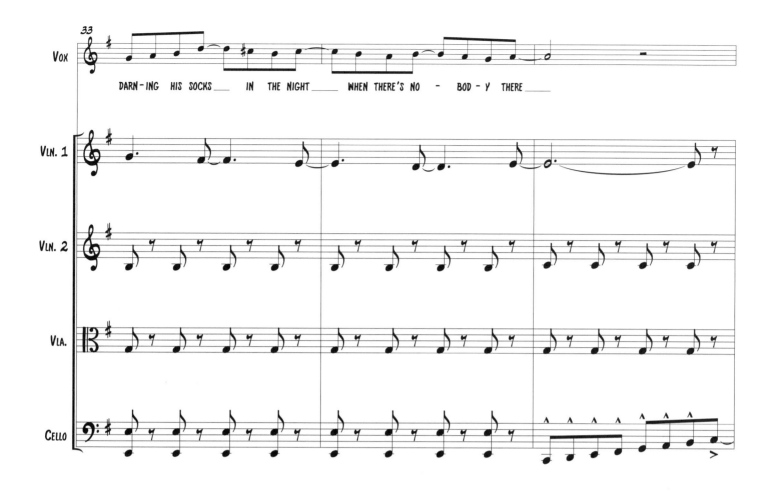

DARN-ING HIS SOCKS___ IN THE NIGHT___ WHEN THERE'S NO - BOD-Y THERE___

WHAT DOES HE CARE___ ALL THE LONE - LY PEO - PLE WHERE DO___ THEY ALL___ COME FROM__

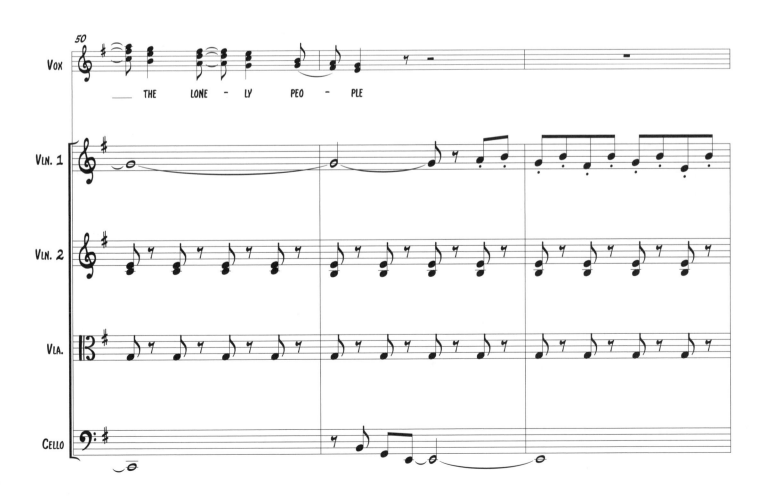

# THE FOOL ON THE HILL

Words and Music by John Lennon
and Paul McCartney

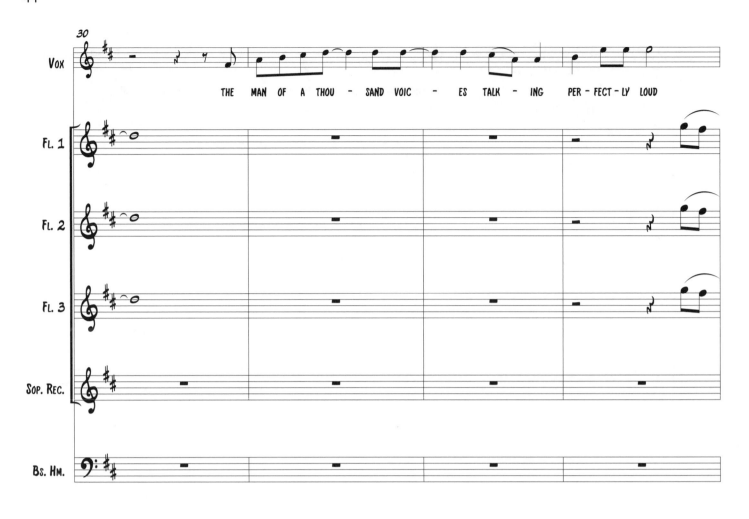

THE MAN OF A THOU – SAND VOIC – ES TALK – ING PER – FECT – LY LOUD

BUT NO – BOD – Y EV – ER HEARS HIM OR THE SOUND HE AP – PEARS TO MAKE

SPIN – NING   'ROUND

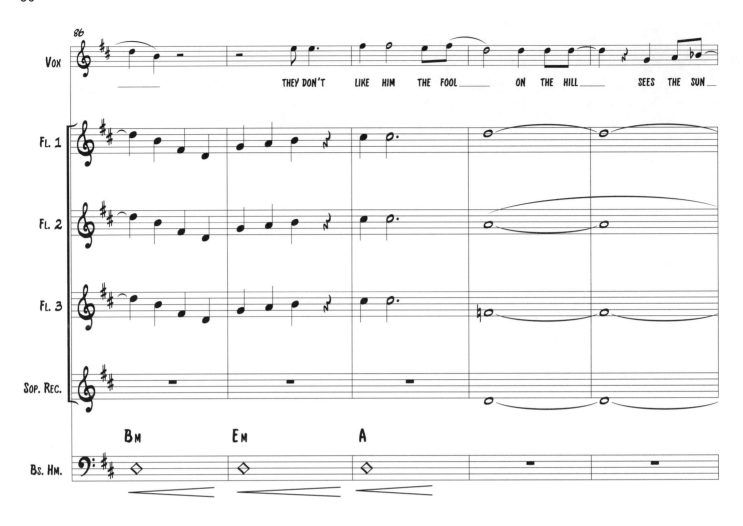

Woah _____ 'round 'round

'round 'round          Oh _____

Fade Out

# GOLDEN SLUMBERS

Words and Music by John Lennon
and Paul McCartney

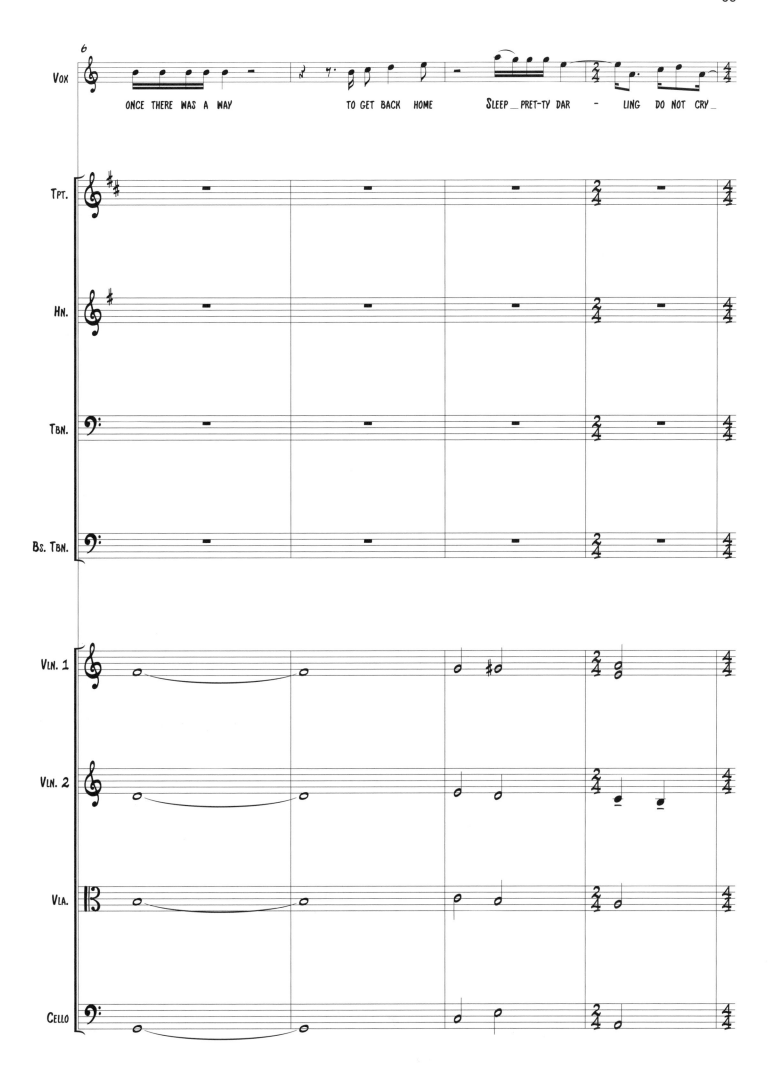

Once there was a way to get back home - ward

SEGUE

# CARRY THAT WEIGHT

Words and Music by John Lennon
and Paul McCartney

Boy, you're gon-na car-ry that weight__ car-ry that weight__ a long__ time

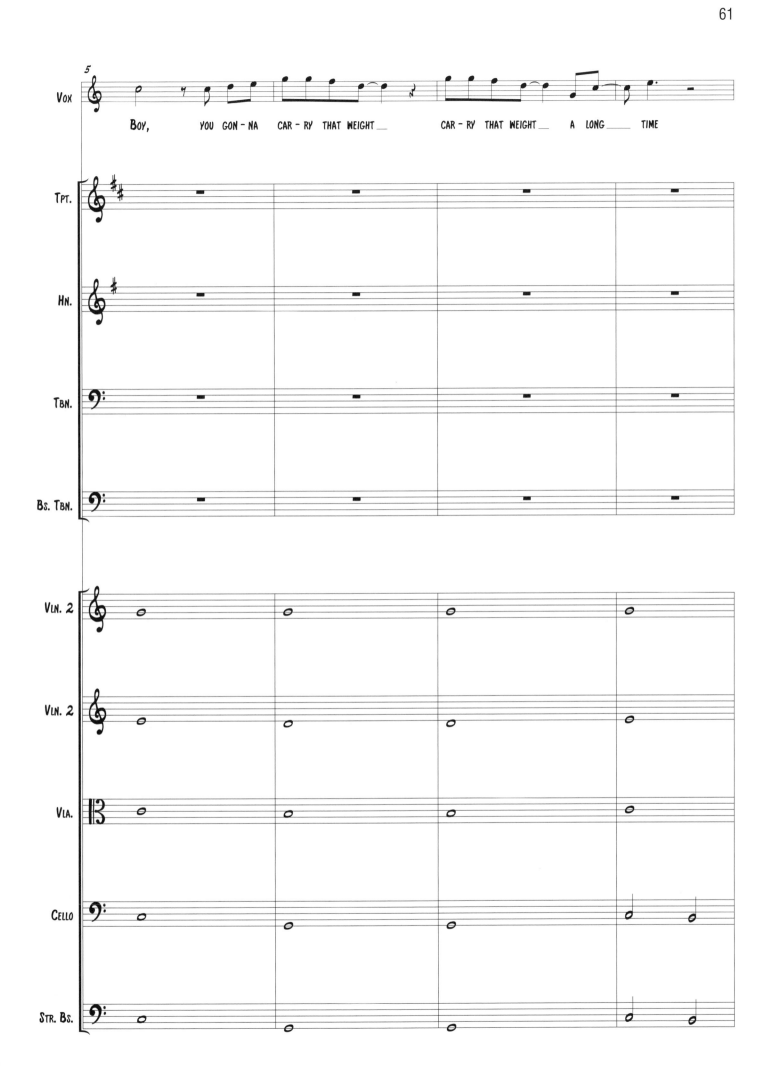

I NEV - ER GIVE YOU MY PIL - LOW

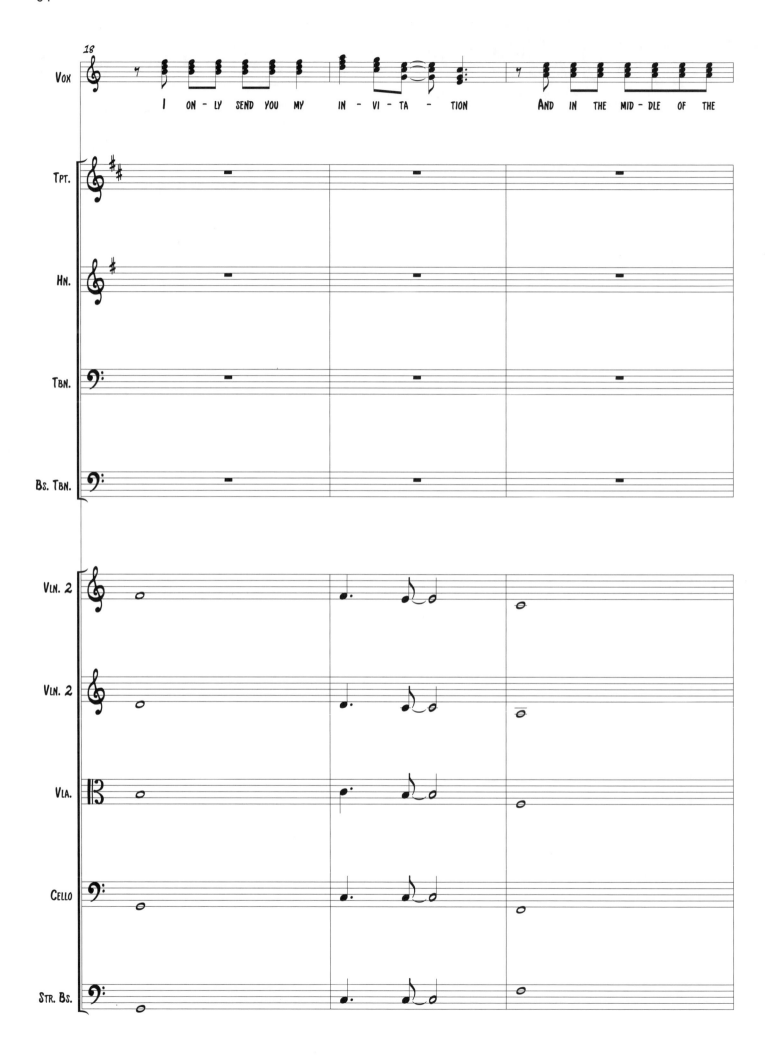

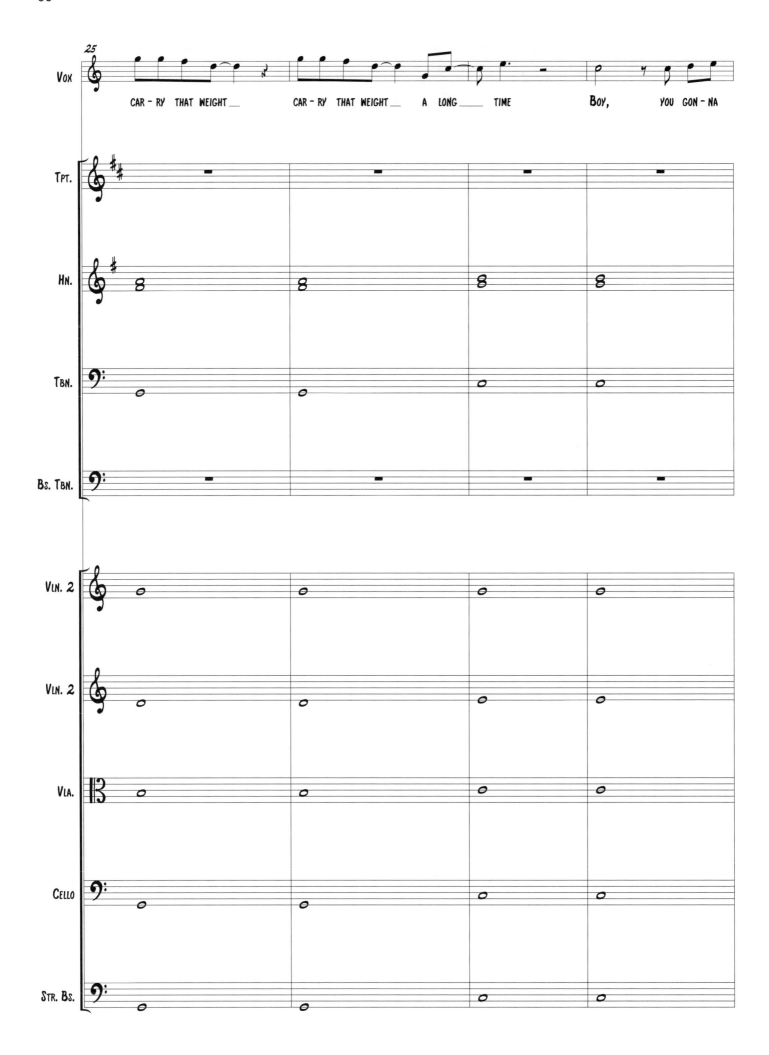

# FOR NO ONE

Words and Music by John Lennon
and Paul McCartney

\* Vocals written in recorded key of B Major.
\*\* Horn written in transposed key of F♯ Major.

# MAGICAL MYSTERY TOUR

Words and Music by John Lennon
and Paul McCartney

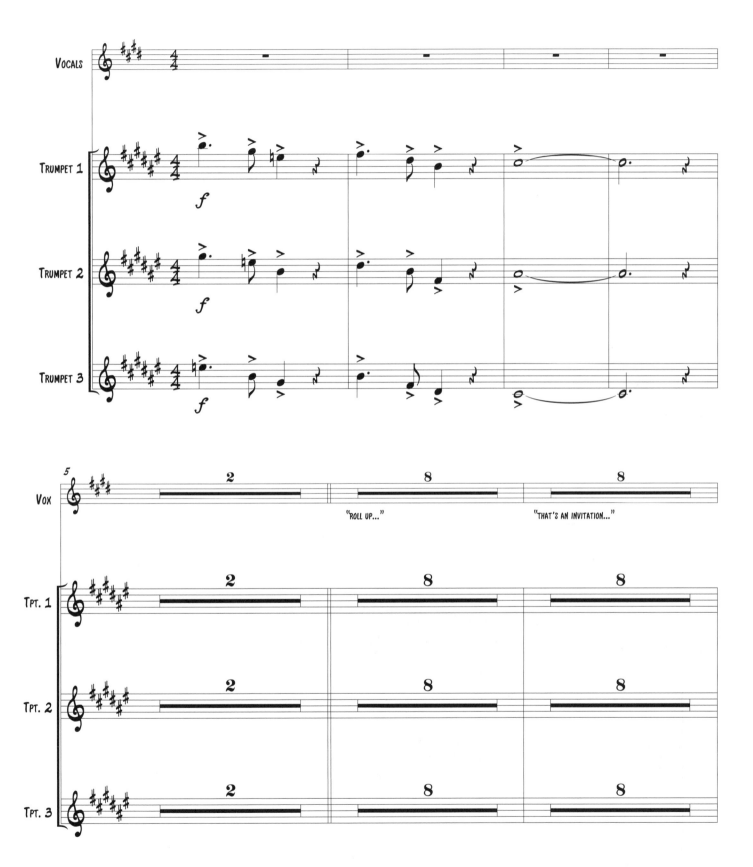

"ROLL UP..."            "THAT'S AN INVITATION..."

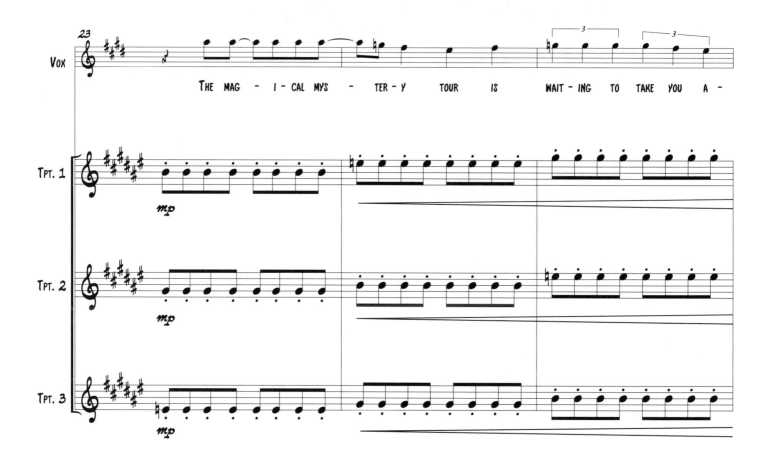

The mag - i - cal mys - ter - y tour is wait - ing to take you a -

way                  wait - ing to take you a - way

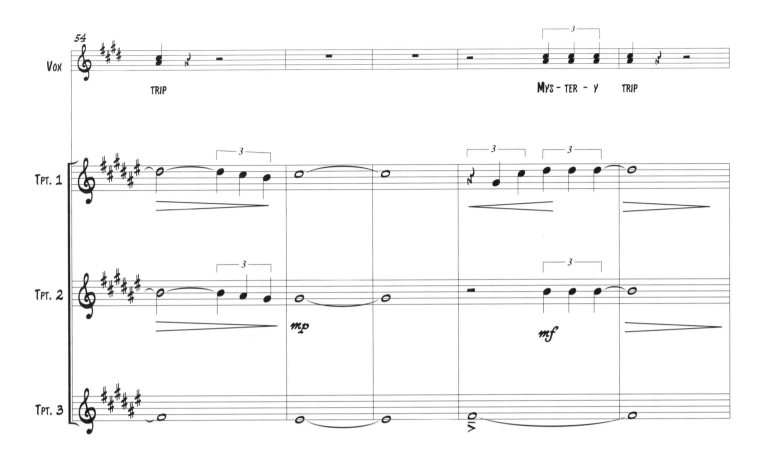

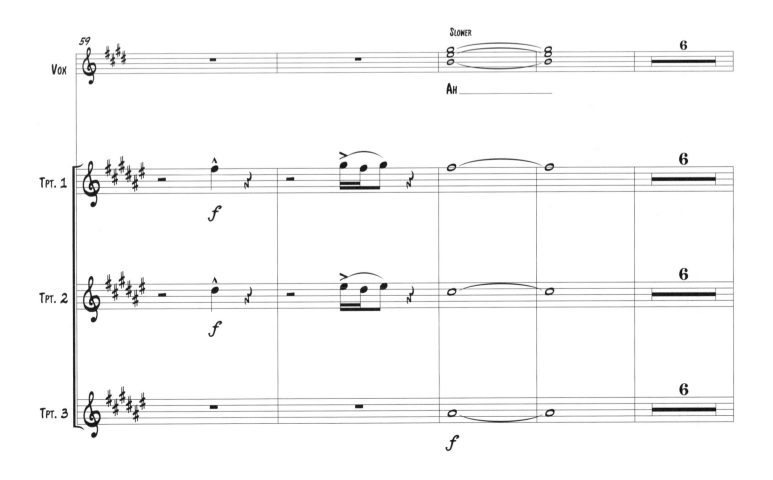

THE MAG-I-CAL MYS-TER-Y TOUR IS COM-ING TO TAKE YOU A-WAY
THE MAG-I-CAL MYS-TER-Y TOUR IS DY-ING TO TAKE YOU A-WAY

COM-ING TO TAKE YOU A-WAY

DY-ING TO TAKE YOU A-

WAY TAKE YOU TO-DAY

(PIANO)

FADE OUT

# GOT TO GET YOU INTO MY LIFE

Words and Music by John Lennon
and Paul McCartney

AN-OTH-ER ROAD___ WHERE MAY-BE I___ COULD SEE AN-OTH-ER KIND OF MIND___

___ THERE _____ Ooo _____ THEN I SUD-

78

Vox: YOU KNEW I WANT-ED JUST TO HOLD _____ YOU _____

Vox: AND HAD YOU GONE ___ YOU KNEW IN TIME _____ WE'D MEET A-GAIN ___ FOR I HAD TOLD _____ YOU _____

I GOT TO GET YOU IN-TO MY LIFE____

I WAS A-LONE____

I took a ride___ I did-n't know what I would find___ there          An-oth-er road___

___where may-be I___ could see an-oth - er kind of mind___ there_____          And___ sud -

FADE OUT

# HELLO, GOODBYE

Words and Music by John Lennon
and Paul McCartney

# I AM THE WALRUS

Words and Music by John Lennon
and Paul McCartney

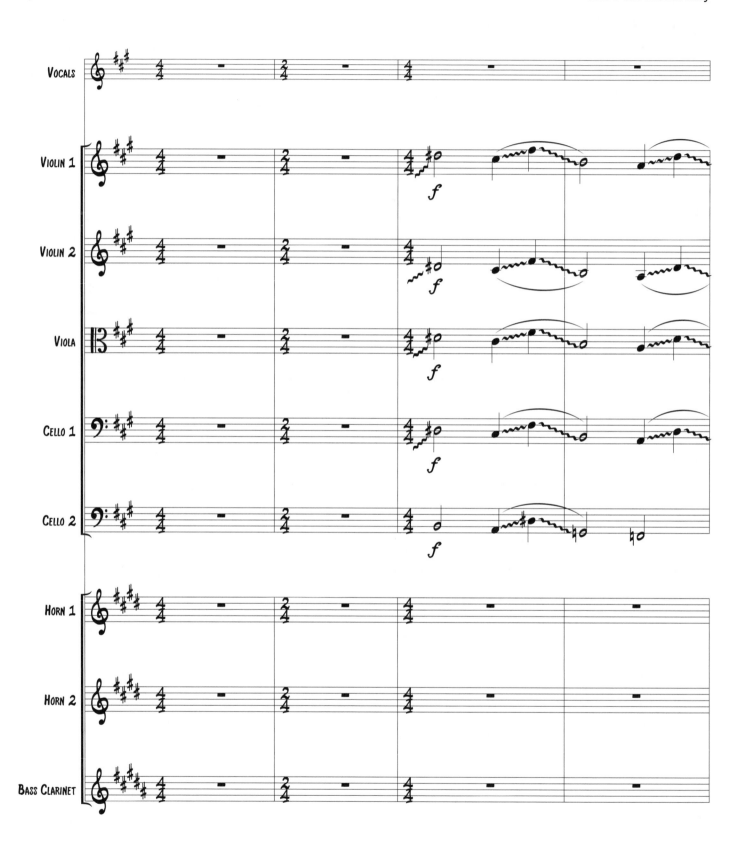

I AM HE AS YOU ARE HE AND YOU ARE ME AND WE ARE ALL TO-GETH - ER

SEE HOW THEY RUN LIKE PIGS FROM A GUN SEE HOW THEY FLY I'M CRY - ING

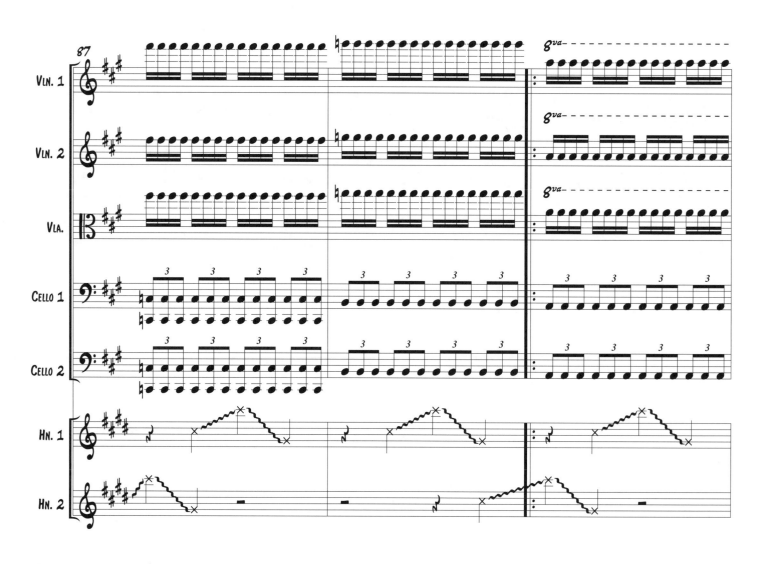

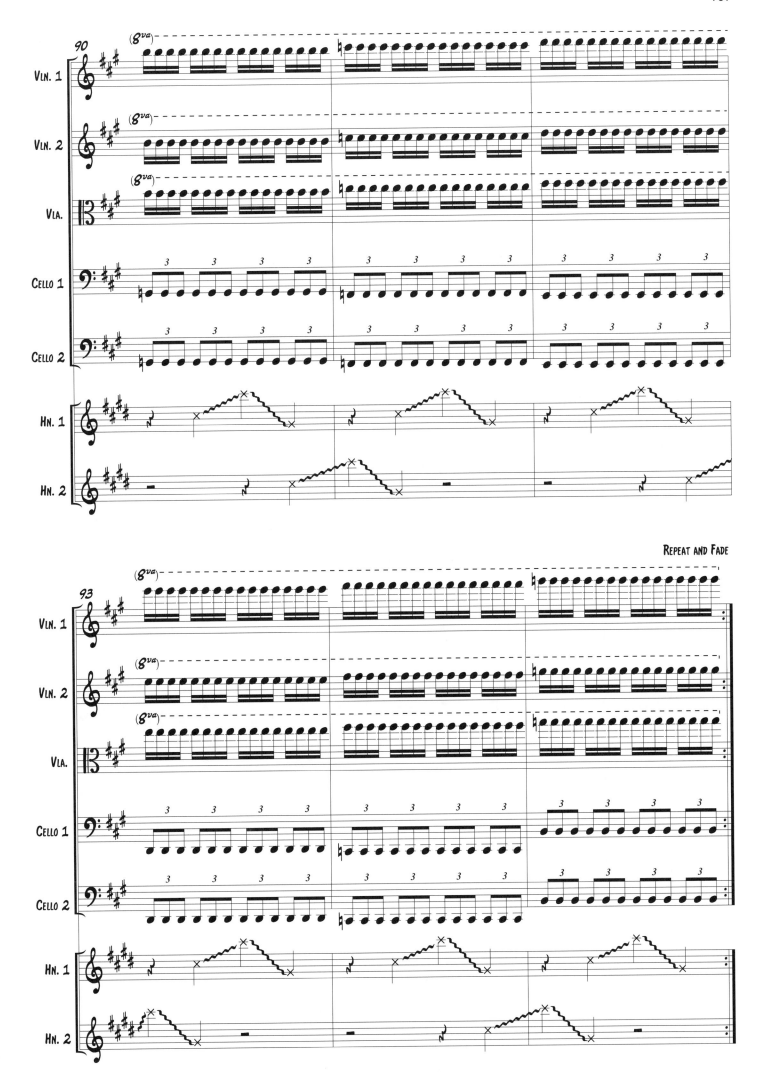

REPEAT AND FADE

# MARTHA MY DEAR

Words and Music by John Lennon
and Paul McCartney

Vox: YOU AND ME___ WERE MEANT TO___ BE___ FOR EACH OTH — ER_____ SIL-LY GIRL_

HOLD YOUR HAND OUT YOU SIL - LY GIRL

SEE WHAT YOU'VE DONE _____ WHEN ____ YOU FIND ____ YOUR-SELF ____ IN THE THICK OF IT

HELP YOUR-SELF __ TO A BIT OF WHAT IS ALL A-ROUND ___ YOU __ SIL-LY GIRL ___

PLEASE ___ BE GOOD TO ME ___ MAR - THA MY ___ LOVE ___ DON'T FOR - GET ___ ME ___

___ MAR - THA MY ___ DEAR ___

# PENNY LANE

Words and Music by John Lennon
and Paul McCartney

122

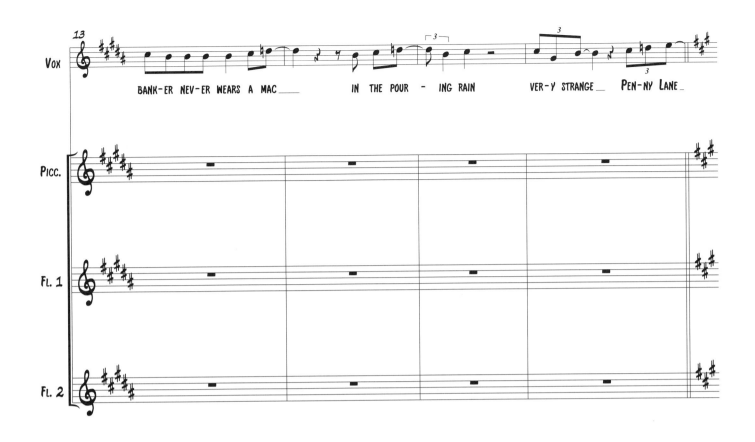

124

# MOTHER NATURE'S SON

Words and Music by John Lennon
and Paul McCartney

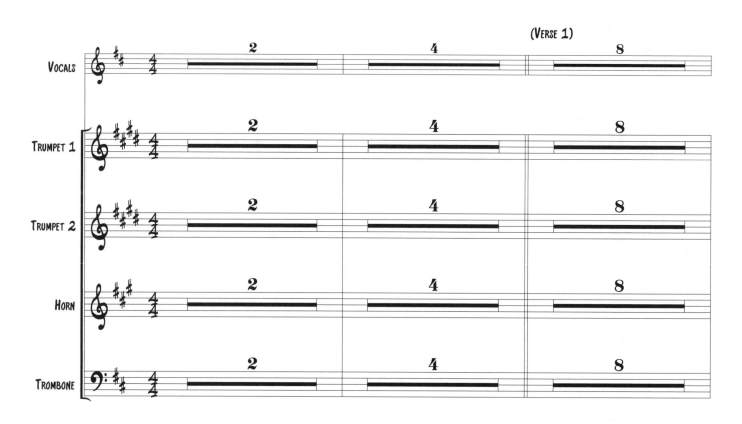

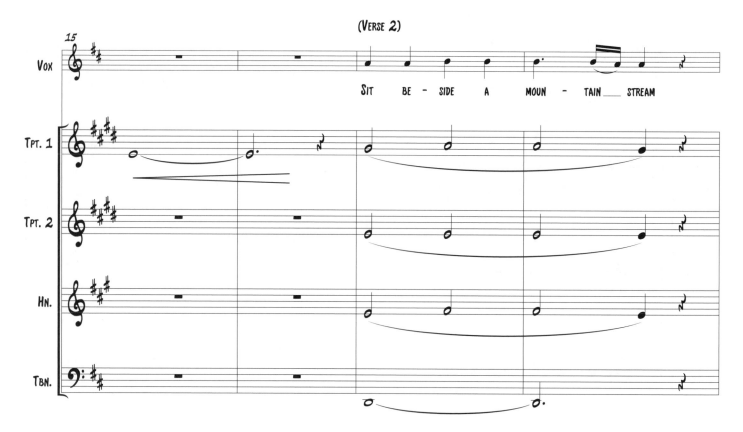

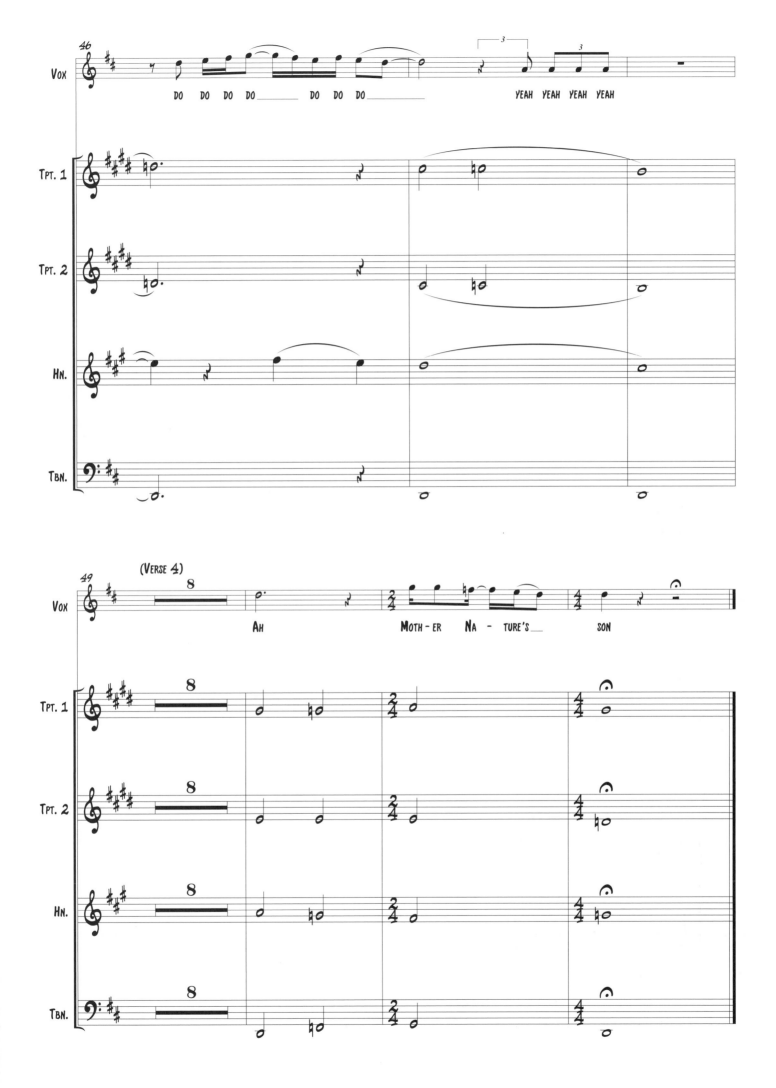

# SGT. PEPPER'S LONELY HEARTS CLUB BAND

Words and Music by John Lennon
and Paul McCartney

# SHE'S LEAVING HOME

Words and Music by John Lennon
and Paul McCartney

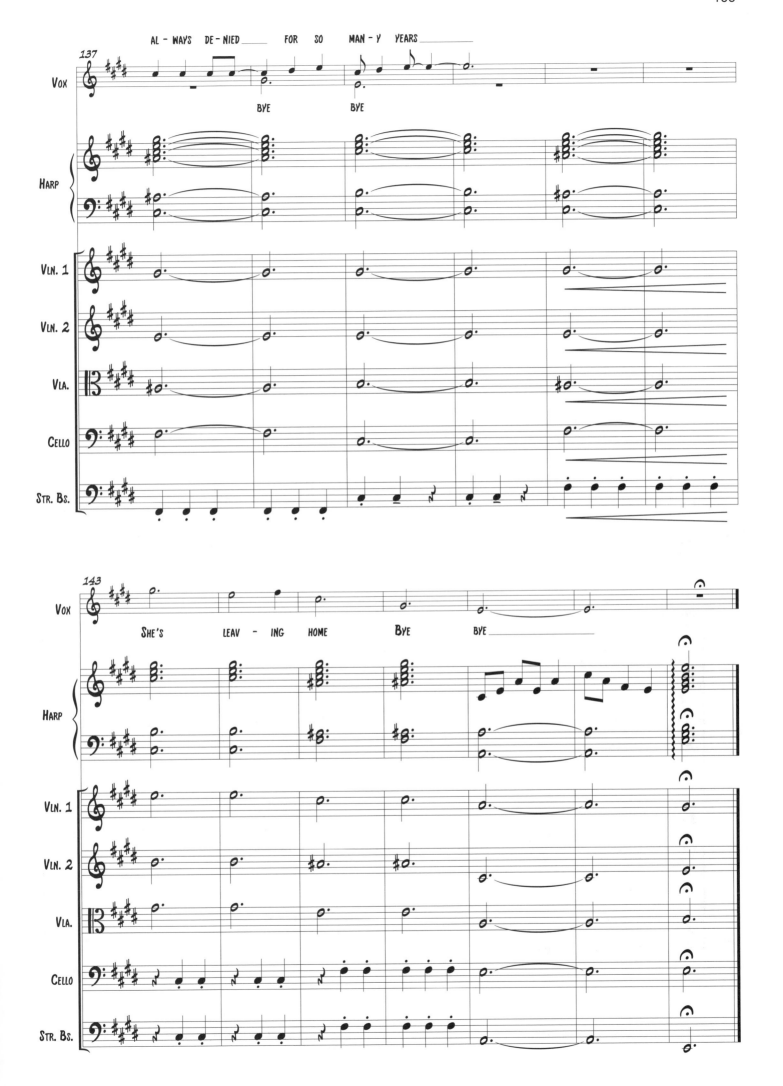

# SOMETHING

Words and Music by
George Harrison

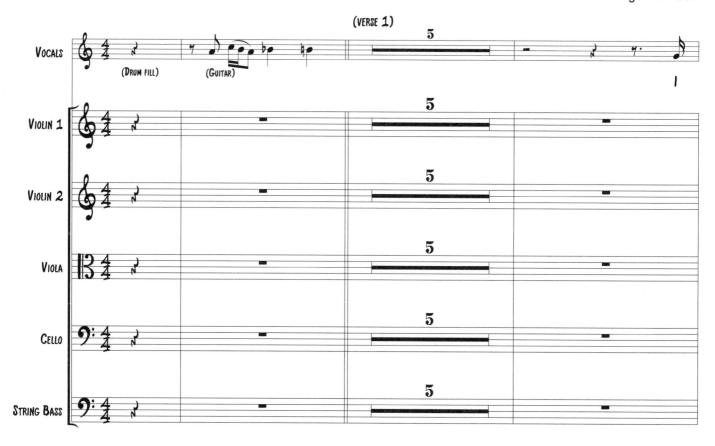

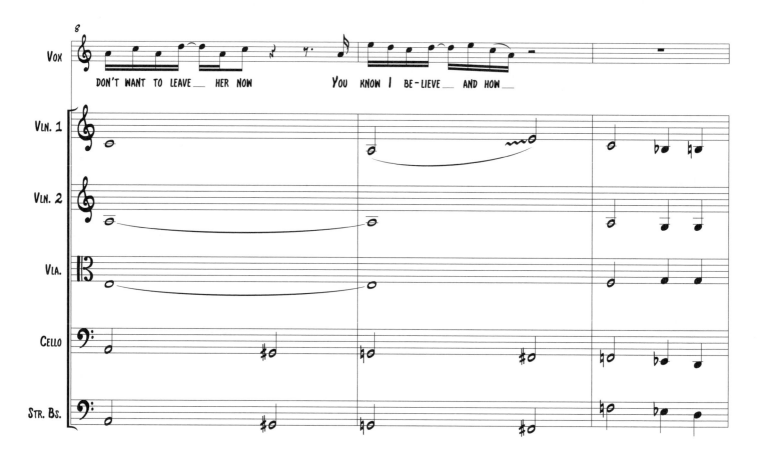

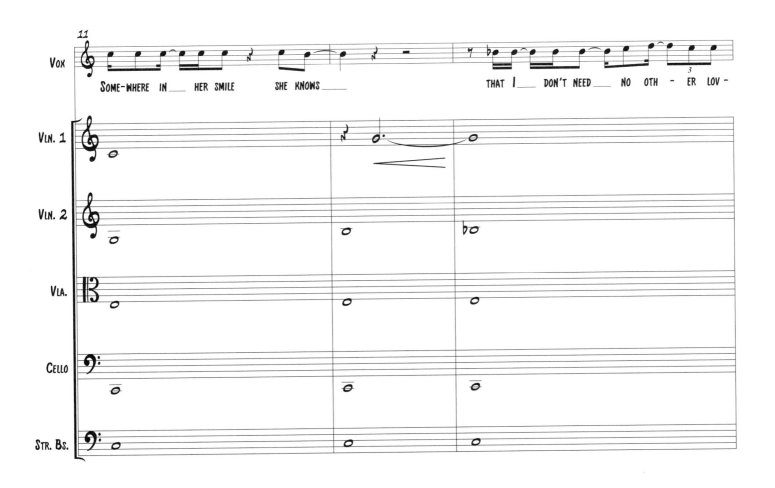

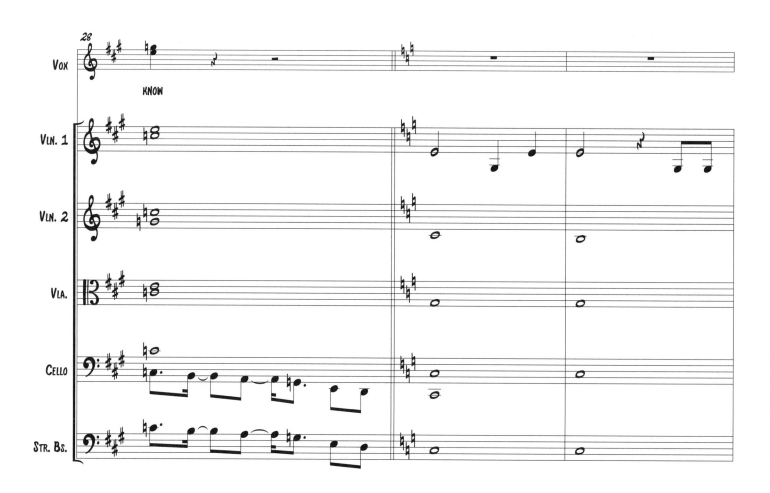

DON'T WANT TO LEAVE__ HER NOW  YOU KNOW I BE-LIEVE__ AND HOW__

# STRAWBERRY FIELDS FOREVER

Words and Music by John Lennon
and Paul McCartney

# WITHIN YOU WITHOUT YOU

Words and Music by
George Harrison

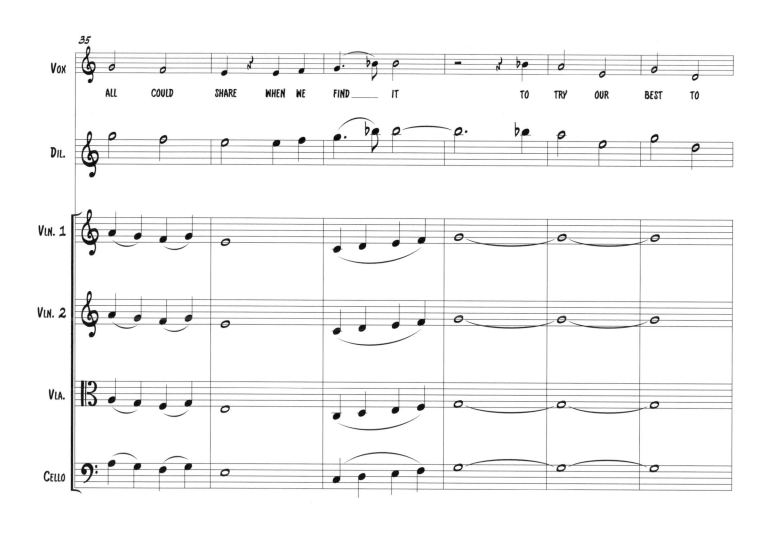

IF THEY ON-LY KNEW

(PERCUSSION)

TRY TO RE-AL-IZE IT'S ALL WITH-IN YOUR-SELF, NO

WHEN YOU'VE SEEN BE - YOND YOUR - SELF  THEN  YOU  MAY  FIND  PEACE  OF  MIND  IS  WAIT - ING

# WHEN I'M SIXTY-FOUR

Words and Music by John Lennon
and Paul McCartney